Douglas County Library
720 Fillmore St.
Alexandria, MN 56308

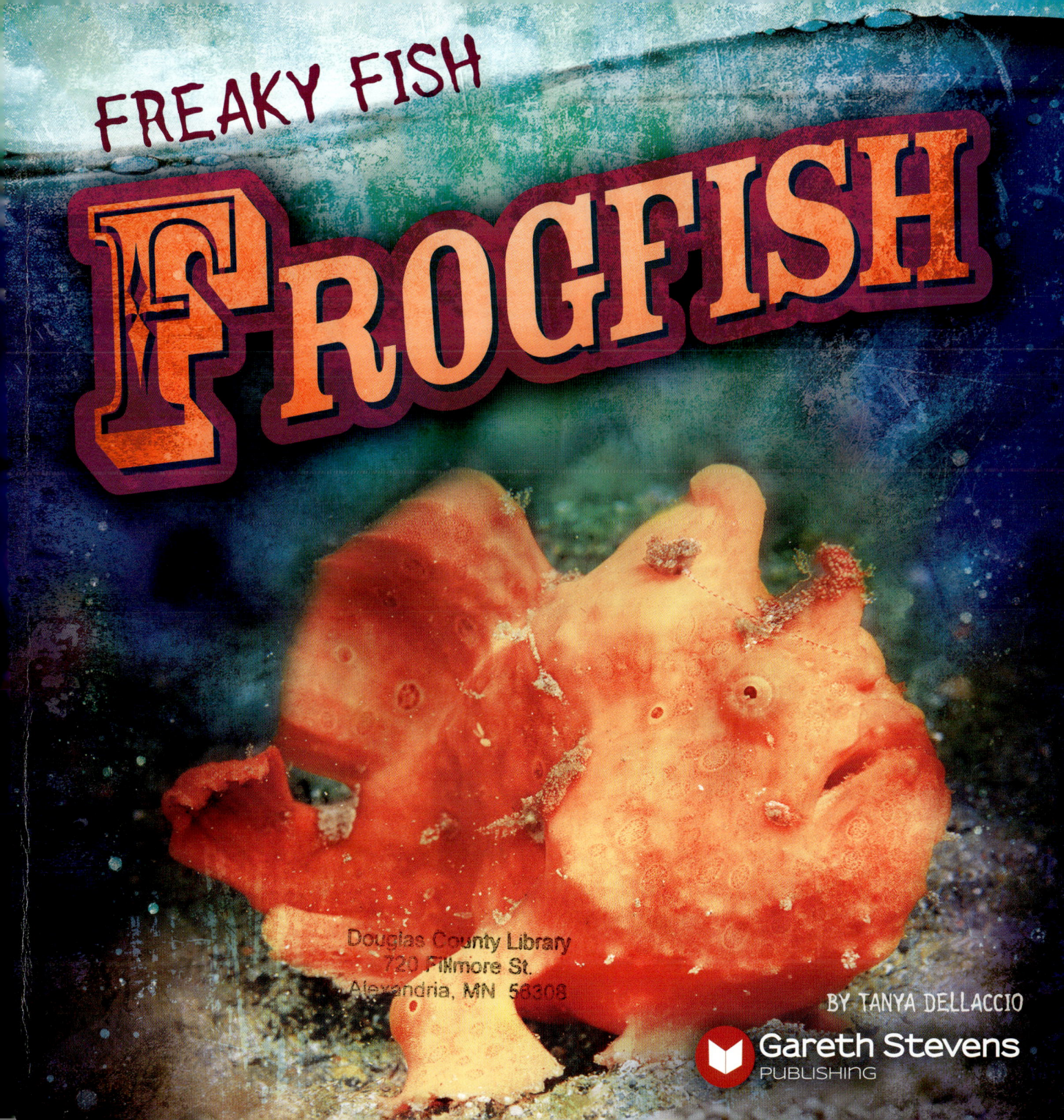

Please visit our website, www.garethstevens.com. For a free color catalog of all our high-quality books, call toll free 1-800-542-2595 or fax 1-877-542-2596.

Cataloging-in-Publication Data

Names: Dellaccio, Tanya.
Title: Frogfish / Tanya Dellaccio.
Description: New York : Gareth Stevens Publishing, 2018. | Series: Freaky fish | Includes index.
Identifiers: ISBN 9781538202654 (pbk.) | ISBN 9781538202593 (library bound) | ISBN 9781538202470 (6 pack)
Subjects: LCSH: Antennariidae–Juvenile literature.
Classification: LCC QL638.A577 D45 2018 | DDC 597'.62–dc23

First Edition

Published in 2018 by
Gareth Stevens Publishing
111 East 14th Street, Suite 349
New York, NY 10003

Copyright © 2018 Gareth Stevens Publishing

Designer: Katelyn E. Reynolds
Editor: Joan Stoltman

Photo credits: Cover, pp. 1, 5 Birgitte Wilms/Minden Pictures/Getty Images; cover, pp. 1-24 (background) Ensuper/Shutterstock.com; cover, pp. 1-24 (background) macro-vectors/Shutterstock.com; cover, pp. 1-24 (background) Kjpargeter/Shutterstock.com; cover, pp. 1-24 (fact box) nicemonkey/Shutterstock.com; p. 7 Michelle Shen/EyeEm/Getty Images; p. 9 Hal Beral/Corbis/Getty Images; p. 10 Borut Furlan/WaterFrame/Getty Images; pp. 11, 19 Rich Carey/Shutterstock.com; p. 13 In Depth Solutions/Shutterstock.com; p. 15 Stubblefield Photography/Shutterstock.com; p. 17 Ethan Daniels/WaterFrame/Getty Images; p. 18 Dr Morley Read/Shutterstock.com; p. 21 (longlure frogfish) Ian Ratcliffe/Shutterstock.com; p. 21 (black hairy frogfish) Wira Wijoga/Shutterstock.com; p. 21 (painted frogfish and striated frogfish) Ethan Daniels/Shutterstock.com.

All rights reserved. No part of this book may be reproduced in any form without permission in writing from the publisher, except by a reviewer.

Printed in the United States of America

CPSIA compliance information: Batch #CS17GS: For further information contact Gareth Stevens, New York, New York at 1-800-542-2595.

Underwater Freak Show.................... 4
Fishing for Food............................. 6
Dinnertime!.................................... 8
The Life of a Frogfish 10
Blending In.................................... 12
Staying Safe.................................. 14
Baby Frogfish................................ 16
A Fish That Walks?......................... 18
Help These Fish!............................ 20
Glossary.. 22
For More Information 23
Index.. 24

Words in the glossary appear in **bold** type the first time they are used in the text.

Underwater Freak Show

Fish, like all other animals, can change over time to survive better in their **environment**. Often, these features make fish look really freaky! One freaky-looking fish that occupies the world's waters is the frogfish.

Frogfish are a group in the anglerfish family. There are about 60 different species, or kinds, of frogfish, each a little different from the others in color, shape, and skin **texture**. These differences help scientists tell the species apart.

FREAKY FACT!

The anglerfish family has around 200 different species. There are three other groups aside from the frogfish in the anglerfish family that make up those species. Each group is just as freaky as the next!

The psychedelic (sy-kuh-DEH-lihk) frogfish gets its name from its wavy stripes of bright orange and white! "Psychedelic" means "having bright, loud colors that seem to move."

5

Fishing for Food

One of the weirdest features of frogfish is on their face. Many frogfish have a long, skinny pole sticking out of the top of their head! This pole is called an illicium (uh-LISH-ee-uhm), and it acts and looks like a fishing pole.

At the end of the "pole" is a very small body part called the esca (EHS-kuh). The esca, like a wiggly worm on the end of a fishing line, moves around to draw animals towards the frogfish.

FREAKY FACT!
The illicium is actually a part of the first **spine** of the back fin on a frogfish. Even freakier, a frogfish is able to grow its esca back if its **prey** gets a good bite!

Animals may think they've found food when they get the esca in their mouth, but it's just a trick. Now, they're close enough for the frogfish to swallow!

ILLICIUM

ESCA

Since most frogfish have an esca to attract prey, they usually just wait for food to come to them. As soon as prey comes close enough, the frogfish opens its mouth and gulps it down!

This can happen in 6 milliseconds, or as quickly as one flap of a honeybee's wing. Frogfish usually eat small ocean creatures, like crayfish or shrimp. But they can also eat larger prey. How? They eat larger prey by stretching their stomach to swallow animals twice their own size!

FREAKY FACT!
All anglerfish, including all frogfish, have some form of **lure** on top of their body, even if it's just a little bump.

A frogfish can open its mouth up to 12 times its normal size when catching food!

The Life of a Frogfish

Frogfish can be found in **shallow** ocean waters near the **equator**. They usually live inside coral **reefs**. Scientists don't know how long frogfish live, especially in the wild. They do know that frogfish in aquariums usually only live a few years, but this isn't a very good way to tell how long they live in their natural ocean environment.

Frogfish come in many sizes. This warty frogfish is tiny!

With a few special tools to help you breathe and see, you can visit a coral reef and see all sorts of beautiful, freaky sea creatures for yourself—like the frogfish!

Blending In

The frogfish's shape, skin, and coloring allow it to blend in to its environment, hiding in plain sight from its predators. Whatever the surroundings, a frogfish will match the plants and animals around it—sometimes by changing color!

Frogfish have soft, lumpy bodies, not smooth shiny bodies like many fish. This shape, combined with their sandy, dull skin, helps to hide them, too. There's a different kind of frogfish for every environment out there, from algae to rocks and sand to coral!

FREAKY FACT!
The hairy frogfish has little spines all over its body that look like seaweed. It's one of the kinds of frogfish that can change colors to blend in better. What a freaky fish!

This hairy frogfish blends right in to its environment. Its skin, shape, and color help it catch prey and hide from predators!

Staying Safe

Even juvenile, or baby, frogfish have a wide range of shapes, colors, textures, and patterns on their body so that they can blend in to eat and hide. Since frogfish are able to hide, or camouflage, so well, battles with predators aren't common.

However, frogfish have a freaky trick for fighting back if they really need to. Some frogfish can fill their body with water if they feel they're in danger, which puffs their body out. This scares away predators!

This juvenile warty frogfish has a lot of growing to do, but it's already great at hiding!

JUVENILE

Baby Frogfish

When a female frogfish is ready to reproduce, or create baby frogfish, her body becomes full of eggs. She swells and begins to float!

The male frogfish pushes her to the surface of the water. Then, she releases, or lets out, her eggs as one big, gooey structure made up of as many as 180,000 eggs, and he releases his male cells. The eggs float there for a few months. A little while after the eggs **hatch**, the babies swim down to the coral.

FREAKY FACT!

Not all frogfish leave their eggs floating on the surface. Sometimes, male frogfish stick the gooey eggs to their side to keep them safe while they grow!

EGGS

The marble-mouthed frogfish is one of several species of frogfish in which the male carries the eggs!

A Fish That Walks?

Because frogfish let their food swim to them, they don't need to move a lot. But when they do decide to move, it looks pretty freaky!

The frogfish doesn't swim like most other fish. Instead, it uses fins on the bottom of its body to walk around the seafloor. The fins act like freaky little feet! If you look close enough at those frogfish walking fins, you'll see they look just like webbed frog feet!

frog foot

The frogfish's four bottom fins make it look like it's walking on all fours like a frog!

19

Help These Fish!

Frogfish are some of the most interesting fish in the world, especially to underwater photographers! But their coral reef home is very easily harmed or killed.

When ocean temperatures rise even the tiniest bit, corals may sicken and die. The entire coral reef **ecosystem**—the home of many amazing species—is affected! Everyone should do their part to keep coral reefs healthy so freaky fish like the frogfish will always have a home.

A FEW FINE FROGFISH

LONGLURE FROGFISH

BLACK HAIRY FROGFISH

PAINTED FROGFISH

STRIATED FROGFISH

21

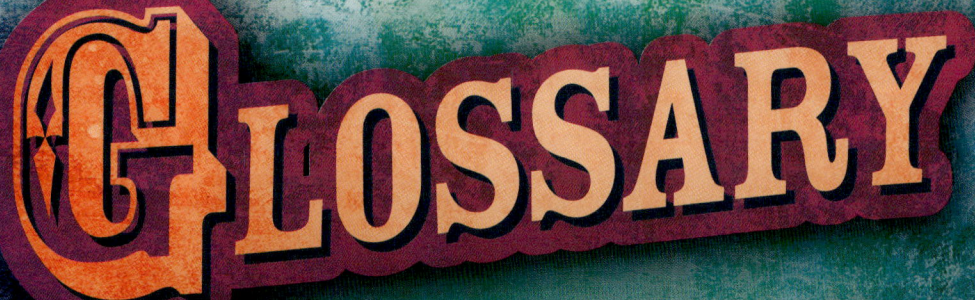

ecosystem: all the living things in an area

environment: the conditions that surround a living thing and affect the way it lives

equator: an imaginary line around Earth that is the same distance from the North and South Poles

hatch: to break open or come out of

lure: an object used to bring an animal closer

prey: an animal that is hunted by other animals for food

reef: a chain of rocks or coral, or a ridge of sand, at or near the water's surface

shallow: not deep

spine: one of many stiff, pointed parts growing from an animal

texture: the structure, feel, and appearance of something

FOR MORE INFORMATION

BOOKS

Leaf, Christina. *Anglerfish*. Minneapolis, MN: Bellwether Media, 2014.

Lynette, Rachel. *Deep-Sea Anglerfish and Other Fearsome Fish*. Chicago, IL: Raintree, 2012.

Wood, Alix. *Ugly Creatures Under Water*. New York, NY: Windmill Books, 2014.

WEBSITES

Frogfish
bbc.co.uk/nature/life/Frogfish
Read more about frogfish behavior and environments!

Hairy Frogfish
kids.nationalgeographic.com/animals/hairyfrogfish/#hairy-frog-fish-face.jpg
Check out these freaky pictures of the hairy frogfish!

Publisher's note to educators and parents: Our editors have carefully reviewed these websites to ensure that they are suitable for students. Many websites change frequently, however, and we cannot guarantee that a site's future contents will continue to meet our high standards of quality and educational value. Be advised that students should be closely supervised whenever they access the Internet.

Index

anglerfish 4, 8
body shape 4, 8, 12, 13, 14
camouflage 12, 13, 14
color 4, 5, 12, 13, 14
coral reefs 10, 11, 12, 16, 20
eggs 16, 17
esca 6, 7, 8
feet 18
fight 14
fins 6, 18, 19
illicium 6, 7
juveniles 14, 15

lifespan 10
mouth 8, 9
predators 12, 13, 14
prey 6, 8, 13
size 10
skin 4, 12, 13
species 4, 17
spines 6, 12
stomach 8